Who Was
Harriet Tubman?

Who Was
Harriet Tubman?

By Yona Zeldis McDonough
Illustrated by Nancy Harrison

Grosset & Dunlap • New York

For my mother, Malcah Zeldis—Y.Z.M.

To Christopher, a Nan's best friend—N.H.

Text copyright © 2002 by Yona Zeldis McDonough. Illustrations copyright © 2002
by Nancy Harrison. All rights reserved. Published by Grosset & Dunlap, a division of
Penguin Putnam Books for Young Readers, 345 Hudson Street, New York, NY, 10014.
GROSSET & DUNLAP is a trademark of Penguin Putnam Inc. Published simultaneously
in Canada. Printed in the U.S.A.

Library of Congress Cataloging-in-Publication Data

McDonough, Yona Zeldis.
   Who was Harriet Tubman? / by Yona Zeldis McDonough ; illustrated by Nancy Harrison.
      p. cm.
Summary: A biography of the nineteenth-century woman who escaped slavery and helped
many other slaves get to freedom on the Underground Railroad.
1. Tubman, Harriet, 1820?-1913--Juvenile literature. 2. Slaves—United States—Biography—
Juvenile literature. 3. African American women--Biography--Juvenile literature. 4.
Underground railroad—Juvenile literature. 5. Antislavery movements—United States—
History--19th century—Juvenile literature. [1. Tubman, Harriet, 1820?-1913. 2. Slaves. 3.
African Americans--Biography. 4. Women—Biography. 5. Underground railroad. 6.
Antislavery movements.]
I. Harrison, Nancy, 1963- ill. II. Title.
E444.T82 M375 2002
973.7'115--dc21

2002004663

ISBN 0-448-42890-3 (GB)   A B C D E F G H I J
ISBN 0-448-42889-X (pb)   A B C D E F G H I J

Contents

Who Was
Harriet Tubman?

No one knows the exact year in which Harriet Tubman was born. It may have been 1820 or 1821. Almost everyone thought the birth of a slave baby wasn't worth remembering. Born a slave, Harriet Tubman grew into a brave and daring young woman. She was brave enough to escape from slavery. She was daring enough to help

others escape, too. Because she led so many to freedom, she was called "Moses." Like Moses in the Bible, Harriet Tubman believed that her people should be free. And she risked her life many times to help them become free. Even after she had escaped safely from the South, she went back to take other slaves north to freedom. Here is her story.

Chapter 1
Life in Maryland

Sometime around 1820 in Maryland, a slave named Harriet Ross had a baby girl. Neither Harriet, who was called Old Rit, nor her husband, Ben, could read or write, so they couldn't record the year of the baby's birth. No one else thought  it was worth doing. But Old Rit loved her tiny child and wanted to protect her. She hoped her little girl, whose nickname was Minty, would learn to sew, cook, or weave. Then she could be a house slave and avoid the backbreaking work picking crops like tobacco, corn, or wheat in the fields.

Old Rit and Ben had been born slaves. They had many children, all of whom were slaves, too. Black people had been slaves in the United States for a long time. Ever since 1619, when blacks from Africa were kidnapped and brought on slave ships

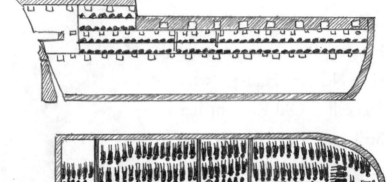

Two Views of a Slave Ship

to Virginia, slavery had been a part of American life. By the early 1800s, most of the Northern states had stopped slavery. But the Southern states had not.

Slaves like Ben and Old Rit worked very hard, yet they were not paid for their work. Instead, Ben and Old Rit lived on land owned by their master, a man named Mr. Brodas. This land and the many buildings on it was called a plantation.

Plantation House

Mr. Brodas' plantation house was large and grand, like so many of those in the South. Ben and Old Rit could see the Brodas' big house every day, but they didn't live there. They lived in a log cabin, like the other slaves on the plantation. Slaves' cabins

were very small. They had no windows. The floors were made of dirt. Piles of worn-out blankets were the only beds. Still, for little Minty, this was home and she loved it.

As soon as she could walk, Minty joined her brothers and sisters and other slave children who were watched by an older slave. The littlest children ran and played naked. The older ones wore a coarse linen garment. None of them wore shoes. Still, they had fun. Summers were warm and bright. They swam and fished in the many streams and creeks.

Even though she was a slave, Minty was happy. She loved her parents. Ben, her father, told her stories about the woods. He could name the birds. He knew which berries were sweet and tasty.

BOUGHT AND SOLD

Slaves brought to the United States from Africa were sold at auction to the person who bid the highest amount of money for them. Groups of black men, women, and children were brought together for this purpose. Auctions were advertised with signs and newspaper ads. White people came beforehand to look over the slaves. They pried open their mouths to check their teeth. They pinched their arms and legs to test their muscles.

Even worse was the way an auction could tear apart a family. A mother might be sold to a plantation owner in Mississippi while her son or daughter might be sold to a plantation owner in Louisiana. The two would never see each other again. Husbands and wives, parents and children, brothers and sisters were cruelly separated.

In 1859, a plantation owner named Pierce M. Butler sold 436 slaves to pay off money he owed. It was the largest slave auction on record in the United States and it was called "The Weeping Time." The slaves, all of whom were born on Butler's plantations, were brought to a racetrack in Savannah, Georgia. They were put in stalls meant for horses while they waited for the auction to begin. By the end of the two-day event, all of the slaves were sold away from the only home they had ever known. They would never see their family or friends again.

Minty's mother told her stories from the Bible. From her mother, Minty learned about Moses. Moses had lived thousands of years before. He led his people, the Hebrews, out of Egypt, where they had been slaves, and into freedom.

Around 1826, when Minty turned six, her life changed. Mr. Brodas hired her out. This meant that she had to leave her parents and her home. She had to go live and work for white people who could not afford to buy a slave of their own. The day she had to leave, a wagon came to take her

away. Minty did not want to go. Her two older sisters had been taken away. She remembered how they cried and cried. But they had to go anyway. So did Minty.

Minty worked for a woman named Mrs. Cook. Mrs. Cook was a weaver. She spent her days in front of a big, noisy loom. Minty helped her wind

the yarn. The air was filled with fuzz and lint. It made Minty cough. She dropped the yarn. She couldn't concentrate. Mrs. Cook got angry. When she was angry, she would punish Minty by whipping her. Slaves were whipped often. That was how the masters made them behave.

Mrs. Cook told her husband that Minty was stupid and slow. So Mr. Cook had her help him instead. He was trying to catch muskrats. He set out traps by the river. It was Minty's job to watch them. It was cold near the river but it was quiet, too. The air was clear and fresh.

Muskrat Trap

One day Minty woke up feeling sick. Mrs. Cook thought she was pretending so she wouldn't have to work. Just as always, Mr. Cook sent Minty out to check the traps. She went down to the river,

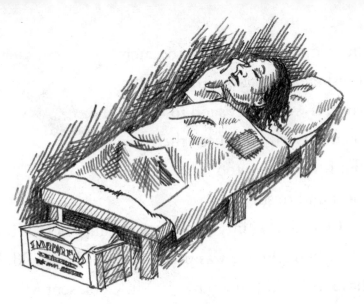

shivering from fever. When she got back, Mrs. Cook saw that she was really sick. She sent Minty home to her parents to get well. Old Rit took care of Minty for six weeks. But then it was back to Mrs. Cook and the loom. Minty could not learn to do the job. The Cooks sent her home again.

Next, Mr. Brodas hired Minty out to a woman named Miss Susan. Minty, who was only about seven, had to watch Miss Susan's baby. If the baby cried, Minty was whipped. At night she sat by the baby's cradle. She rocked it gently. But Minty was tired. She would fall asleep and the baby would begin to cry. Then Miss Susan would get angry at being woken, and Minty was whipped again. Minty learned to stay alert for the baby, but it was hard. She was always tired.

Once, when Miss Susan's back was turned, Minty reached for a lump of sugar that was in a

bowl on the table. She had never tasted sugar. Slaves were rarely given candy or treats. It looked so good. But Miss Susan saw her. Furious, she reached for the whip. Minty was too fast. Out the door she flew. She did not stop running until she was sure Miss Susan was no longer chasing her. But now what? If she went back, she would face a whipping.

Minty found a pigpen. She crawled inside to hide. She was very young, but she was bold. She tried to fight the piglets for potato peelings and other scraps of food. But the mother pig pushed Minty away.

After five days, Minty was filthy and starving. She knew she would have to return to her mistress. Later Minty would say, "I didn't have anywhere else to go, even though I knew what was coming."

NAT TURNER'S REBELLION

Born around 1800, Nat Turner was a slave in Southampton County, Virginia. When he was little, his mother told him that he would one day lead his people to freedom, like Moses in the Bible. She had memorized verses and whole chapters of the Bible, and she taught them to her son.

Turner grew up to be a preacher. Other slaves called him The Prophet, which means "teacher." He was a silent, moody man who spent a lot of time alone. Turner believed what his mother had told him: that he had been chosen to lead his fellow slaves to freedom.

In 1828, Turner announced that there would be a certain sign letting him know it was time to rebel. On August 20, 1831, there was an eclipse of the sun. Turner thought that was the sign. He led a band of slaves from plantation to plantation, killing the whites they met. Wherever they stopped, more slaves joined them. Soon, there were seventy slaves who killed sixty white people in all. The rebellion was broken up with the help of Federal troops. One hundred blacks were killed putting down the rebellion. But Turner was not among them. He stayed hidden in a cave for two months. Later he was found, and on November 11, 1831, Nat Turner was executed.

Instead of being hired out again, Minty was sent back to Mr. Brodas. Now Minty had to work in the fields, which was very hard. She split logs, loaded wood onto wagons, worked the plow, and drove oxen. Minty had grown strong and sturdy. She could do the jobs. And when she was in the fields, she could see the sky and feel the wind. The other slaves talked while they worked. That was how Minty began to hear new ideas. She heard

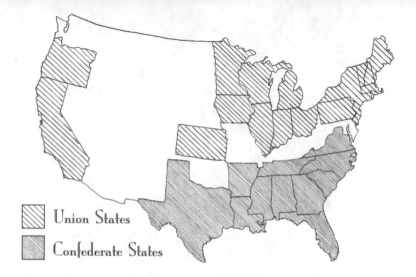

Union States

Confederate States

slaves who said they wanted to be free. Some of them escaped from the plantation.

They went north, to freedom. Others, like Nat Turner, started rebellions to end slavery. Nat

Turner was caught and killed. But his ideas didn't die. More and more, slaves thought about being free. Late one day in 1834, Mr. Brodas' slaves gathered with the slaves from another plantation to shuck the corn. They sang while they worked, peeling the pale green husks from the golden ears of corn. One slave stood apart. Minty watched him. He began moving across the big field. At first the overseer—the man who kept the slaves in line—didn't notice. The slave was halfway across when the overseer saw him. He shouted for him to return. The man kept going.

The overseer followed, holding his big whip. Minty followed, too. The overseer was running now, chasing the escaped slave. The slave ducked

into a store. The overseer ran after him. The slave was cornered in the store. The overseer called to Minty. He wanted her to help him tie up the runaway slave. But Minty didn't move. She stood watching the two men. Suddenly, the slave pushed past the overseer and was out of the store. Gone.

As for Minty, she blocked the doorway, so the overseer couldn't follow the slave. The overseer picked up a heavy, two-pound weight and threw it at the runaway. The weight missed the runaway slave, but it hit Minty on the forehead. She fell,

unconscious and bleeding.
She was brought to Old Rit,
who nursed her tenderly.
No one thought Minty
would live. Still, Old Rit
cared for her daughter night
and day. Eventually, Minty recovered from the
wound, though it left a scar on her forehead.

It wasn't just the scar that made Minty different
now. People treated her with respect. Although she
was only thirteen or fourteen, she had defied an
overseer. No longer was she called by her childhood name of Minty. Instead, she was called
Harriet, her mother's name. Clearly, she was not a
child anymore.

Chapter 2
Looking for the North Star

Harriet was not the same after she got well. She suffered from headaches. Sometimes she had sleeping spells. One minute she might be awake and talking. The next, she would be sound asleep. The spells frightened her. She heard a rumor. Mr. Brodas, her master, was going to sell her. He would sell some of her brothers, too. What would happen

to her? She might be sent farther south, to New Orleans, Louisiana, or Natchez, Mississippi, in a chain gang.

In a chain gang, the slaves were chained together at the ankles to prevent their escape. The trip south would be long and hard. If Harriet fell asleep in the road, the overseer would whip her. He might whip her very hard and leave her to die. Her brothers would not be able to save her.

Even if she could survive the trip, Harriet knew that being sold some place farther south was a bad thing. That was where so many of the cotton plantations were.

COTTON AND TOBACCO

Plantation owners in the South grew many different kinds of crops, which they could sell for money. Two of the most popular were cotton and tobacco.

Cotton was used for cloth and clothing. The plantation owners needed many workers to plant and pick the cotton. First the slaves had to pick the little balls of cotton from the cotton plants. Then they had to clean the cotton balls to make them ready for spinning. Slaves toiled long and hard to do this back-breaking job. Tobacco was another commonly grown crop. Slaves were also used to plant and pick tobacco.

The owners of the big plantations knew that without slaves working for them, they would not be able to grow the crops that brought in their money. They told themselves that slavery was all right, because they needed the workers. But the wealth enjoyed by the plantation owners was made from the blood and sweat of the slaves who worked for them.

Cotton Plant

Tobacco Plant

Working in the cotton fields was very hard work. Also going farther south meant she would be further from the Northern states. Further from freedom. Harriet did not want to be a slave all her life. She wanted desperately to be free.

Harriet began to pray that Mr. Brodas would die. To her amazement, he did get sick and died soon after. And Harriet found that she was sorry.

She believed it was wrong to have prayed for his death. But now she had a new owner who was more fair. His name was Dr. Anthony Thompson. Dr. Thompson hired Harriet and her father out to a builder named John Stewart.

At first she swept, dusted, washed clothes, and made the beds in Mr. Stewart's house. But she

hated the work and asked if she could work outside with the men. Mr. Stewart agreed. Harriet worked alongside the men, cutting down trees and splitting logs. She was a good worker. Sometimes Mr. Stewart let her take other jobs. She even earned some money for her work. She had to give

Mr. Stewart part of the money, but she could keep some of it. Harriet looked for more outdoor work—hauling logs, driving an ox cart, plowing fields.

Harriet worked five years for the builder. She became even stronger and more capable. She was more than twenty-one years old now—all grown up. Her father kept teaching her things, too. He taught her to move through the woods without making a sound. He showed her how to find the

North Star, near the Big Dipper. The North Star was a guiding light for slaves. It showed the way north—the way to freedom.

Ben told his daughter that, with the North Star in sight, you would know you were headed in the right direction. But what if there were cloudy nights and the stars were hidden? Ben told his daughter to feel the trees for moss. Moss grew only on the north sides of trees. Even without the North Star, the moss could help a traveler. Harriet listened to what her father had to say. She remembered his words. In time, they would help her.

Chapter 3
A Free Man's Wife

In 1844, when she was about twenty-three, Harriet fell in love with John Tubman. John's parents had been slaves. But their master freed his slaves at the time of his death, so John was born free. John and Harriet made plans to marry.

Harriet began making a quilt. She sewed it

from different scraps of cloth. Sewing was hard work. She wasn't used to holding the needle. It was so small. Again and again, she dropped it. It was hard to find a needle on the dirt floor. Still, she kept working until the quilt was done. The finished quilt had many colors: yellow, purple, white, and green. It was the most beautiful thing she had ever owned. When she married John and went to live in his cabin, she took the quilt with her.

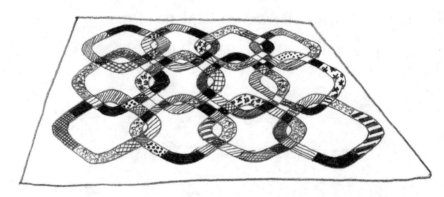

John was happy with their life. He loved Harriet and liked the money she made. They had a cabin of their own. Life was good. But Harriet was not so content. What if her new owner wanted to sell her?

She and John would be separated. She still thought about escaping. She begged John to go north with her. They would follow the North Star. In the North, Harriet would be a free woman. They would both be free.

John did not want to leave home. It was too dangerous. What would they eat? How would they

ABOLITIONISTS

Abolitionists were eighteenth- and nineteenth-century reformers who believed slavery was evil and wanted to end—or abolish—it. Unlike other anti-slavery supporters, who worked towards a gradual end of slavery, abolitionists called for slavery to end immediately. Although the Quakers had long opposed slavery, abolitionists were not just Quakers, but people of other religions as well.

The abolitionist movement started in 1780, in England, when William Wilberforce and his followers spoke out against the African slave trade. The American abolitionist movement began in 1831, when William Lloyd Garrison started *The Liberator*, an antislavery newspaper, in Boston. Other abolitionist newspapers and books followed. But it was not until after the Civil War ended in 1865 that the Thirteenth Amendment, outlawing slavery in the United States, was passed.

William Lloyd Garrsion

live? He told Harriet to put escaping out of her mind. She could not. She told him about the dreams she had. Dreams of freedom.

John told Harriet that if she tried to escape, he would tell the master. After that, Harriet began to fear her husband. John did not share her dream. If she wanted to be free, she would have to go north without John.

One day Harriet was working in a field close to a road. A white woman drove up in a buggy. She wore the plain clothes of a Quaker. She began to talk to Harriet. She asked Harriet her name and

how she got the scar on her forehead. Harriet knew Quakers didn't believe in slavery. She could talk to the white woman. She could trust her. The woman came again on other days. If no one was watching them, they spoke. She told Harriet that if she ever needed help, she could ask her.

In 1849, bad news came to the plantation. Harriet and some of her family were to be sold. Sold! Now she had to escape. She told her brothers. They made a plan.

QUAKERS

Started in England in 1648, the Quakers were a Christian religious group founded by George Fox. They got their name because of Fox's demand that they "tremble at the word of the Lord." Quakers wore plain clothes and led simple lives. Their possessions were few. They were strongly opposed to war. Their religion did not allow them to fight. There are still Quakers today, who worship in Quaker meeting houses, without ministers or priests. Instead, each member of the group is allowed to speak at the meeting.

Equality is a very important part of the Quaker way of thinking. Because Quakers were such strong believers in equal rights for all people, they were very opposed to slavery. During the nineteenth century, many Quakers were also abolitionists. They helped slaves escape and offered their homes, stores, stables and barns as "stations" on the Underground Railroad. They risked their own safety and freedom to help other people who were not free.

George Fox

That night, she waited until John was asleep. Then she went to meet her brothers. They moved through the woods. How much noise her brothers made! They grew frightened. Escape was too risky. They were going back. Harriet had to come with them. She said no. She would go alone. But they would not let her. She tried to fight them. They were bigger and stronger. They forced her to return.

In two nights, a slave trader would be coming for Harriet and her brothers. Harriet faced a hard choice. If she stayed, she would be put on a chain gang. She would probably die on the long walk south. But if she escaped, who would go with her? Not her husband, John. Not her brothers.

She decided to run away all by herself. She went to bed as usual. When John was asleep, she

got up. Packing was easy. She put a little salt pork and cornbread in a bandana. She took the quilt she had made. She didn't dare take more. Harriet slipped out of the house. Finally, she was on her way to freedom, on her way north. Harriet was going to make her dream come true.

Chapter 4
Free at Last

Harriet walked through the dark woods. She moved without making a sound. Ben had taught her well. Ben also told her that bloodhounds could not follow a scent through water, so she waded through streams whenever she could. Finally, she came to house of the Quaker woman. The Quaker woman let her in. But she told Harriet it was not safe for her to stay. Harriet would have to leave that night. The Quaker woman told her what to do next. Harriet was grateful. She wanted to thank the woman. But how? Harriet gave the wedding quilt to her and said good-bye.

Harriet had a long trip ahead of her. First she followed the Choptank River in Maryland. When it got light, she hid. When it was dark, she started moving again. The river was forty miles long. And it was only the start of her trip. Slowly, Harriet kept going. When the river ended, she followed a road to Camden, Delaware. She looked for a white house with green shutters. The Quaker woman had told her to do this. The woman in the white house was named Eliza Hunn. She let Harriet stay with her for three days. She gave her new clothes and food for the trip. Then Harriet set out again.

Harriet had become a traveler on the Underground Railroad. The Underground Railroad had no tracks or cars but it had a series of "stops"—homes or stores of Quakers and abolitionists— where runaway slaves could find shelter.

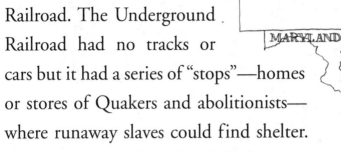

The Underground Railroad had its own special code words to trick the white slave owners. Escaping slaves might be called "bundles," "parcels," or "packages." "One bale of cotton" might mean one slave. "Two small bales" might mean that the escaping slaves were children.

Slave hunters were everywhere. They got rewards for bringing back runaway slaves. Harriet knew her master would be looking for her. She used her bandana to cover her scar. She traveled at night. Sometimes she dressed as a man or as a fancy lady with a veil. In these clothes, she was safer. Finally, she reached Pennsylvania.

Pennsylvania was a free state.

Now Harriet was a free woman.

Later, Harriet said how she felt: "I looked at my hands to see if I was the same person now that I was free. There was such a glory over everything, the sun came like gold through the trees and over the fields and I felt like I was in heaven."

But freedom was not easy. Years later, Harriet said, " . . . I was free, but there was no one to welcome me to the land of freedom. I was a stranger in a strange land . . ." It was true. Her home, her family, and her friends were back in Maryland. One day, she would go back to get them.

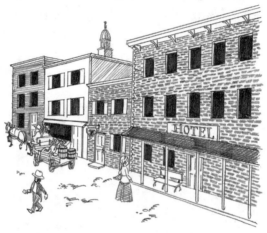

Harriet took a job cooking and cleaning in a Philadelphia hotel. She did not like the work but compared to being a slave, it was easy. All the money she earned was hers. And if she truly hated her job, she could leave it. No one could force her to stay.

VIGILANCE COMMITTEES

As more slaves escaped from the South, vigilance committees sprang up in the larger towns and cities of the North, such as New York, Philadelphia, and Boston. These committees, like the one William Still worked for, raised money to help the runaways. They gave food, shelter, and money to the escaped slaves, who often arrived with torn, filthy clothes, bare feet, and nowhere to go. The members of the vigilance committees also helped the runaways settle into communities by giving them letters of recommendation and finding jobs for them.

William Still

After work, Harriet began to visit the offices of the Philadelphia vigilance committee. This was a group of people who helped runaway slaves. The men and women there sometimes had news of Harriet's family back home. Harriet learned that her sister Mary and Mary's family were going to be sold.

Harriet decided she had to go back to Maryland. Her sister's family needed her. She would bring them north. William Still was the secretary of the vigilance committee. And he was her friend. He warned her not to go. It was too dangerous. But she wouldn't listen.

A clever plan was devised. Harriet's Quaker friends got the plan to John Bowley. He was married to Harriet's sister, Mary. John was a free man, although his wife and children were slaves.

By the time John got the plan, his family had already been taken to the slave auction. But they had not been sold yet. It was lunchtime, and the auctioneer was taking a break. He would sell the rest of the slaves after he had eaten.

Right then, John Bowley walked to the slave pen. In his hand, he held a large white envelope with a message inside. He handed it to a guard watching the slaves. The message said that Mary's master already had a buyer for her and the children. John was to take Mary and their children to the inn where the auctioneer was having lunch.

The message was a trick. It was not from Mary's master. But the guard did not suspect anything. John took Mary and the children. Quickly, they went down the street. But they did not go to the inn to find the auctioneer.

They were escaping! In the middle of the day!

They tried to walk calmly so as not to attract attention. Finally, after what seemed like a long

walk, they came to a house with a picket fence. Inside was a Quaker man. He was the one who had written the message. The Quaker took the family up to his attic.

Night came. The family crept out and into a wagon. The Quaker man covered them with blankets and drove them to a river. A fishing boat, filled with blankets and food, was waiting for them. John sailed the boat up the Chesapeake River in Maryland. He was told to sail toward Baltimore. He had to look for two lights, one blue and one yellow. John sailed all night long. As morning came, he worried. How would he see the lights in the daytime? But he did and guided the boat to them.

A white woman was on the shore, sitting in a wagon.

"Who are you?" she asked.

"A friend with friends," John answered, for this was the code phrase he had been told to say. The woman greeted him warmly  and helped the family into her wagon. She covered them with blankets and bags of onions and potatoes. Next she drove them to a stable, where they got out of the wagon and waited until dark. Then she helped them back into the wagon and drove them to a brick house in Maryland.

The white woman knocked on the door and then they all went inside. There was Harriet, waiting for them! She had arranged for the boats and for the wagons.

Now she was ready to lead them north.

John and Mary saw that Harriet had a pistol. She had bought it with the money she earned. Armed with the gun and her knowledge of the swamps, Harriet led her sister's family from station to station on the Underground Railroad. They hid during the day and traveled at night. At times they walked; at other times they went by boat or wagon. Finally, they arrived safely in Philadelphia. It was the first time Harriet had been a conductor on the Underground Railroad, but it was certainly not the last.

Chapter 5
The Conductor

Harriet planned to go south again. She had many relatives who needed her help. But the trip was even more dangerous after 1850. That was because the Fugitive Slave Law had been passed. Now runaway slaves who had reached free states had to be sent back to their masters. And if people

did not turn in runaways, they could be fined or put in jail. Runaway slaves could be shot, whipped, or sold to the deep South, where they would probably die anyway.

If Harriet wanted to make sure her "parcels" reached safety and freedom, she would have to take them across the U.S. border to Canada. There was no slavery in Canada. But the closest towns in Canada were much farther north than Philadelphia

CANADA

UNITED STATES

or New York. The trip would be longer. There would be greater risk of discovery. Slave hunters were on the lookout. Rewards were offered for turning in slaves, and the slave hunters wanted to collect them. Still, Harriet was determined to make the trip.

Harriet went back to Maryland in 1851. She led one of her brothers and two other men to freedom. Up north, she took a job in another hotel. She worked hard and saved her money. She was going south again. This time, she would bring her husband, John Tubman, with her. She traveled to the plantation where she used to work. She was

wearing a man's suit. A man's hat hid her scar. But when she reached John's cabin, she had a surprise. John had another wife now. He wouldn't go with her.

Harriet quickly left. She gathered another group of slaves together. They wanted to be free, so she led them north. Before there had always

been family members in her group along with other slaves. But after this she began taking groups of people she didn't know.

Harriet set up a routine. In the winter, she rented a house in St. Catherine's, Canada. Other former slaves lived with her. They chopped wood to earn money. In spring and summer, she went to Cape May, New Jersey, or Philadelphia. There, she earned money working in hotels. Twice a year, in the spring and fall, she went south. Each time she did, she brought back more slaves to Canada. Sometimes she taught other slaves how to escape on their own. She drew maps in the dirt, described the landmarks, and told them where to get help.

By now Harriet had lots of experience. While she never traveled the same route twice, she grew familiar with the swamps, rivers, and potato holes along the way. She knew all the Quaker meeting houses where "passengers" could find shelter.

She used many tricks to help runaways avoid

slave hunters. Men dressed like women. Women dressed like men. Slaves escaped on a Saturday night. Sunday was not a workday. The slaves would not be missed until Monday. Slave owners wouldn't be able to organize their search parties or print their wanted posters until Monday. By then Harriet and the other passengers would be long gone.

People began to talk about Harriet. They made up stories about her: She could see in the dark, sniff danger in the wind, carry a grown man for miles. The stories were not true, but people still told them. Slave owners knew about Harriet, too. They put up posters promising big rewards for her capture. At one point, there was $40,000 in rewards being offered.

Harriet learned about the posters, which described her age, height, and scar. The posters said she couldn't read or write. Once, in a train station, Harriet heard two men talking about her. They were trying to decide if she was the woman in the poster. Harriet was carrying a book.

She opened it and pretended to read. The men decided that she was not the woman on the poster. Harriet had tricked them, but barely. She was lucky she had not been holding the book upside down.

Then Harriet heard that her father was in trouble with his master. Harriet knew what she had to do. She would go back and get her parents. But Ben and Old Rit were not like her other passengers. They were old and frail. They could not walk all night or wade through rivers. She would have to find another way.

Harriet returned to the plantation in Maryland  in 1857. She found an old horse named Dollie Mae. Luring the horse to the woods, Harriet tied her to a tree. Then she made a crude wagon from old carriage wheels, an axle, some boards, and some rope. Now she was ready to get her parents. They could ride to Canada.

Harriet rode with them part of the way, but it became too risky for her to ride out in the open. She got out and went the rest of the way on foot. In St. Catharine's she met her parents again. For the first time, they were free. Harriet found them a house in Auburn, New York. Now part of her money went to support Ben and Rit. She had several different jobs.

Sometimes, she spoke at antislavery meetings to make extra money. At first, Harriet was shy in front of a crowd. But she was a good storyteller. People liked to hear about her narrow escapes. Soon she became an excellent speaker. She traveled to different cities to give her speeches.

In 1860, Harriet was on her way to Boston to give a speech. She stopped to visit a relative in Troy, New York. Trouble was brewing. A former slave, Charles Nalle, had been caught by a slave hunter. Nalle waited at the courthouse for his hearing. Many people were there. Some were for slavery. Others were against it. The judge decided

Nalle had to return to his master. The crowd was furious. A riot broke out and Harriet got involved. She risked her own life to help Nalle escape. When her wounds had healed, she went on to Boston to make her speech.

Later that year, Harriet made one final trip to the South. She brought a family with two small children to the North. After that, Harriet's friends in the antislavery movement convinced her to

stop. She could no longer be a conductor on the Underground Railroad. The slave owners wanted her dead. Harriet was worth too much alive. She would have to find another way to work for freedom.

Chapter 6
A Country at War

In 1861, Civil War broke out between the Northern and the Southern states. There were many reasons for the war. One of them was slavery. The South wanted to keep its slaves. People in the North wanted to end slavery throughout the United States. So the South decided to secede—or pull away—from the North. The eleven Southern states formed their own army. They called themselves the Confederate States of America. The North didn't want the South to secede. The North went to war to make the Southern states rejoin the Union, which is what the North called itself.

Confederate Flag

Union Flag

John Andrew, the governor of Massachusetts, asked Harriet to work for the Union army. Andrew had heard Harriet speak. He knew about her life as a slave. He knew about her work on the Underground Railroad. He believed she could help the Northern cause.

Here was another way for Harriet to work for freedom. She said yes. The first thing she did was travel to Port Royal Island off the coast of South Carolina. Thousands of Northern soldiers were

stationed there, waiting to fight. So were thousands of runaway slaves. By law, the slaves were not yet free, but they wanted to join the Northern army. They wanted to help fight for their freedom.

But there were problems. The slaves still thought and acted like slaves. They expected the

white soldiers to give them orders. They were not used to thinking or acting like free men. That's where Harriet came in. She taught the slaves to see themselves as free people. She taught the soldiers to work with the slaves.

Harriet also helped black women. She taught them how to make things that they could sell. She helped them find ways to earn a living as free people in the North, not as slaves in the South.

Many of the slaves in Port Royal were sick or hurt. Often their owners had wounded them, trying to prevent their escape. A hospital was set up for them on the island.

Harriet became a nurse. She cleaned wounds. She put cool cloths on the foreheads of patients with high fevers. Flies buzzed around the

wounded patients all day long. Harriet shooed them away.

Some of the patients had dysentery. Dysentery caused horrible stomach cramps. Most people who caught it died. Harriet remembered the medicines from certain roots and herbs her mother used to make. Would they help her patients? Harriet wanted to find out. She went to the woods, gathered water lilies, and pulled up their roots. She

Water Lilies

Crane's Bill

hunted for crane's bill. She boiled these plants into a strong brew. There was a man dying of dysentery. Harriet gave him some of the brew to drink. In a few days, the man began to get better. People thought it was another one of Harriet's miracles. If she was at your bedside, you would not die.

The war dragged on into 1862 and beyond. For a while it seemed as if the South would win. Hundreds of thousands of soldiers, both Northern and Southern, were wounded or killed. Still, neither side would give in. The bloody fighting continued.

In 1863, President Abraham Lincoln issued the Emancipation Proclamation, which freed the slaves in the Confederate states. Southern black men could join the Northern army. They formed their own all-black regiments. They had wanted to help the Union cause and now they could.

Abraham Lincoln

Still, the war did not end.

Along with the black regiments, there was a new role for Harriet. Colonel James Montgomery asked if she could be a scout for his black

olonel James Montgomery

troops. In effect, he was asking her to be a spy. Harriet was a perfect choice. As a small, black woman, she looked harmless. She could slip behind enemy lines and approach the blacks who were with their masters in the Confederate army. These blacks would trust her. They might share information about the Southern army. This information could help the Union cause.

Harriet became Commander of Intelligence Operations for the Union Army's Department of the South. Nine scouts were under her command.

She was in charge of an area that went from South Carolina to Florida. Though the white men she led weren't used to reporting to a black woman, they quickly came to respect and admire her.

Being a spy was dangerous work. But Harriet was used to danger. She used her knowledge of the rivers to help lead an invasion. On June 2, 1863, General Montgomery, Harriet, and about three hundred black soldiers set out along the Combahee River in South Carolina. Their aim was to knock out the railroad tracks that ran by the river's edge.

They also wanted to destroy the bridges that crossed it. By destroying bridges and tracks, the

Southern troops could not get supplies. Without food, guns, and first-aid supplies, the South could not win the war.

Harriet and the others traveled in the dark night until they reached a bend. Harriet told the pilot of the boat to stop. There was a camp of Confederate soldiers nearby. Quietly, the men got out and surrounded the camp. They captured the Southern soldiers without firing a shot.

More Northern gunboats came up the river. The Southern soldiers saw them and called for help. Harriet's men were too quick for them. They set fire to their food supplies and their cotton.

They also set fire to their big plantation homes. Many slaves were still working on the plantations. When they saw the black soldiers, the slaves rushed to join them.

The Union gunboats finally turned around and headed back. The raid was over. The Union won the battle, and 756 slaves had joined their Union forces. With more and more men on their side, the Union had a better chance of winning the war.

Harriet continued to lead Union troops into enemy territory. She always carried her pistol and was not afraid to use it. But she still wore a long skirt. It got in her way. However, she could not dress in men's clothes, the way she had done before.

THE COMBAHEE RIVER INVASION

Dressing in men's clothes wasn't considered proper. Ladies were supposed to wear long skirts and lots of petticoats underneath them. What a bother.

Then Harriet heard about Amelia Bloomer. Mrs. Bloomer had designed "a sensible costume for females." The costume was made up of a small jacket, short skirt, and full trousers. Harriet wanted one. As she said, "I made up my mind [that] I would never wear a long dress on another expedition. . . but would have a bloomer as soon as I could get it."

Harriet worked as a spy for two years. By 1864, she was tired. She wanted to go back home to rest. She also wanted to see her parents.

FREDERICK DOUGLASS

A great speaker and important leader in the abolitionist movement, Frederick Douglass was born a slave in Maryland around 1817. As a boy, he secretly taught himself to read and write. This was an extremely dangerous thing to do. Had he had been caught, he could have been put to death. After his escape from slavery in 1838, Douglass began giving lectures about his life. He was a powerful and brilliant speaker. Many people came to hear what he had to say. Then, in 1845, he wrote and published *Narrative of the Life of Frederick Douglass*. In it, he described the many cruelties slaves were forced to endure, like whippings and beatings.

Because the book revealed his master's identity, Douglass had to flee to England, where sympathetic supporters bought his freedom. Back in the United States, Douglass published an antislavery paper, *The North Star*. During the Civil War, he was an advisor to President Abraham Lincoln. He also helped recruit black soldiers for the Union Army, and worked to make sure that newly freed blacks had the right to vote.

Douglass published two other books, *My Bondage and My Freedom* (1855) and *Life and Times of Frederick Douglass* (1881). He served in several government posts, including minister to Haiti. He died in Washington, in 1895.

The government still owed her $1,800 for her work. Though many of Harriet's important friends—including the famous black speaker, minister, and leader Frederick Douglass—wrote to the government for her, she was never paid the money.

When she was sure her parents were well, and after she had gotten back her own strength,

Harriet returned to work. She went to Fortress Monroe Hospital in Washington, D.C. There she cared for black patients. Soon she was promoted to

CONSTITUTIONAL AMENDMENTS

The men who wrote the Constitution in the 1700s knew that the country would change in the future. The government had to find a way to deal with these changes. So they provided a way to make changes to the Constitution: amendments. This meant that lawmakers could vote to add certain important new laws.

Since the 1700s, Congress has added many new amendments to the Constitution. These amendments reflected the changing needs and attitudes of the American people. The Thirteenth, Fourteenth, and Fifteenth amendments were all passed in the years after the Civil War. These amendments put an end to slavery and guaranteed the right of citizenship to all people, regardless of their race or color.

Abraham Lincoln

Head Nurse. In April 1865, the Civil War ended. The Union army had won the war. There would be no more Confederacy, but instead a single and united nation, the way it had been before all the fighting.

In December 1865, slavery was finally abolished throughout the United States. Not only had Harriet lived to see it, she had helped to make it happen.

Chapter 7
Moses of Her People

Harriet went back to her house in Auburn, New York. Her parents were old and needed her. Other former slaves came there for her help, too. Even though blacks were free, their troubles had not ended. They still did not have the same rights

as white Americans. For instance, blacks were not allowed to live in white neighborhoods, shop in stores owned by whites, or worship in churches that white people attended. Black children could not go to school with white children. They went to schools just for blacks. Lots of white people would not hire black people to do a job. Many former slaves were poor or sick. They had no way to earn a living and nowhere to go. Harriet took them all in. She never said no.

Harriet needed money to care for these people. How would she earn it? Help came from a white

woman named Sarah Bradford. Sarah visited
Harriet in Auburn. Harriet told her many stories
about slavery and helping people escape.

Even though she had never learned to read or
write, Harriet had an excellent memory. She
remembered the smallest details. And because she
had memorized passages from the Bible, the way
she told these stories was filled with drama and
poetry. She told about her many trips on the

Underground Railroad, the war, and her work as a nurse and a spy.

In 1869, Sarah Bradford published Harriet's biography. It was called *Scenes in the Life of Harriet Tubman*. All the money it earned would go to Harriet.

That same year, Harriet married Nelson Davis. They had met when he was fighting for the North in one of the black brigades. Nelson was a handsome man twenty years younger than Harriet, but he had come down with tuberculosis, a disease that affected the lungs. He needed caring for, too.

Harriet's first husband, John Tubman, had been killed in Maryland in 1867. Harriet had never really had the chance to make a home or raise a family with him. Nelson gave her another chance. After he got better, he worked as a brick-layer. The money he earned helped support the people in Harriet's care.

Harriet always had more stories to tell. And she always needed money.

So Sarah Bradford wrote another book, *Harriet Tubman: The Moses of Her People.* It was published in 1886. More money came from the new book but, still, there never seemed to be enough.

In 1888, Nelson Davis died. Harriet's parents had died a few years earlier. Now she was all alone

again, but she kept working. She was already caring for several poor, old, or sick black people in her own home. But to care for more people, she needed a bigger house and more land. Not content with what she was doing, she dreamed of something bigger: a hospital and rest home for any black man or woman who needed it.

Harriet earned money by raising vegetables on the land she owned and selling them door-to-door. When she stopped at a house, she was often invited inside. Sometimes she was offered her favorite drink—a cup of tea with butter. Sitting at the table and sipping the tea, she spun her tales from the past. She would describe a Civil War battle with these words: "And then we saw the lightning, and that was the guns; and then we heard the rain falling, and that was the drops of blood falling; and when we came to get the crops, it was dead men that we reaped." Or she might talk about President Lincoln, who had been assassinated in

1865 by John Wilkes Booth. She remembered how an old man had responded to the death by saying, "We kneel upon the ground, with our faces in our hands, and our hands in the dust, and cry to Thee for mercy, O Lord, this evening." Sometimes she went even further back in time, telling stories she had heard in her own childhood, about the old slave ships that brought Africans to America, stories about the whips, chains, and branding irons.

Another way Harriet earned money was by giving speeches. Once she was asked to speak along with the famous women's rights workers, Susan B. Anthony and Elizabeth Cady Stanton.

The two women had worked together for years. They were working to prove that women were equal to men. They also worked to get women many new rights, including the right to vote. In the nineteenth century, only men could vote. Harriet was a good example of how women were

TWO OF A KIND: ELIZABETH CADY STANTON AND SUSAN B. ANTHONY

Elizabeth Cady Stanton met Susan B. Anthony at the first national Women's Rights Convention, held in Seneca Falls, New York, in 1848. The two became good friends and partners. Both believed women deserved rights equal to those of men. They wrote books and articles, gave speeches, and worked to spread their message of equality. They wanted to make sure women earned as much as men for doing the same jobs, and that women could own property. Most important, they wanted women to have the right to vote. It was not until 1920—years after both had died—that all women in the United States could vote.

SUSAN B. ANTHONY

ELIZABETH CADY STANTON

equal to men: Couldn't she do all the things a man could do and more? Standing in front of the audience, she said, "I was the conductor of the Underground Railroad for eight years, and can say what most conductors can't say. I never ran my train off the track and I never lost a passenger."

Then Harriet learned that the land across from her house was about to be sold. Here was her chance. She didn't have enough money, but a bank loaned her what she needed. Now she could make her dream come true. She moved the men and women she cared for into one of the two houses on the new property.

Soon, people from all over came to the house. They read about Harriet's life and wanted to meet her. She had many interesting visitors. People wrote to her, too. She received a letter, a medal, and a black silk shawl from Queen Victoria in England.

Yet Harriet still had money worries. In 1903, she turned her house over to the African Methodist Episcopal Zionist Church. She would still live in the house, but the church would pay the bills. Yet Harriet, who had never asked the people who lived with her for any money, didn't like certain changes made by the church. She said,

"When I gave the Home over to Zion Church, what do you suppose they did? Why they made a rule that nobody should come in without a hundred dollars. Now I wanted to make a rule that nobody could come in unless they had no money. What's the good of a Home if a person who wants to get in has to have money?"

Harriet was an old woman now. Still, she liked taking walks through town. When she couldn't walk anymore, her grandnieces and grandnephews pushed her in a wheelchair. At the age of 92, she could no longer go out, but people still came to see

her. And even though she could not read herself, she still had someone read her the newspaper every day.

In the spring of 1913, Harriet caught pneumonia. She knew she would not get well. With one of her brothers and some good friends at her side, she died. The town of Auburn decided to honor her. People gathered in the Auburn Auditorium. Flags flew at half-mast. Many speakers praised the work she spent her life doing. A bronze plaque was placed on the front entrance of the Auburn Courthouse in her memory. It says, "With rare

courage, she led over three hundred Negroes up from slavery to freedom."

Harriet will always be remembered for her courage, for her strength, and, most of all, for her fierce devotion to the freedom of her people.

TIMELINE OF HARRIET'S LIFE

1821 —— Harriet "Araminta" Ross is born around 1821 in Maryland

1827 —— At age six, Harriet is hired out to work for the Cooks

1834 —— When Harriet helps a slave to escape, she is hit in the head with a two-pound weight

1844 —— Harriet falls in love with and marries John Tubman

1849 —— Harriet escapes to freedom

1850 —— The Fugitive Slave Law is passed, making Harriet's trips on the Underground Railroad even more dangerous

1851 —— Harriet returns to Maryland to help one of her brothers and two other men escape

1857 —— Harriet helps her parents escape to freedom

1860 —— Harriet is injured in Troy, New York, helping former slave Charles Nalle avoid being sent back to his master
Harriet makes her final trip South to help other slaves escape

1861 —— Harriet begins work as a nurse and teacher of former slaves for the Union army

1863 —— Harriet becomes a scout for the Union army
Harriet and General Montgomery capture an entire camp of Southern soldiers

1864 —— Harriet leaves the army because of exhaustion

1867 —— Harriet's first husband, John Tubman, dies

1869 —— Harriet's biography, *Scenes from the Life of Harriet Tubman,* is published
Harriet marries Nelson Davis

1886 —— The second book about Harriet, *Harriet Tubman, The Moses of Her People,* is published

1888 —— Harriet's second husband, Nelson Davis, dies

1903 —— Harriet turns her house over to the African Methodist Episcopal Zion Church

1913 —— Harriet catches pneumonia and dies in Auburn, New York

TIMELINE OF THE WORLD

The Missouri Compromise occurs: Missouri is admitted to the U.S. as a slave state, but slavery is barred in the rest of the Louisiana Purchase — **1820**

Joseph Niépe produces the first photographs on a metal plate
The first U.S. railway is constructed in Massachusetts — **1826**

The refrigerator is invented — **1834**

Samuel F. B. Morse patents the telegraph — **1844**

The California Gold Rush begins — **1848**

California becomes the 31st state of the U.S. — **1850**

Herman Melville publishes *Moby Dick* — **1851**

The United States Supreme Court rules that slaves are not citizens — **1857**

Pony Express mail service begins between St. Joseph, Missouri, and Sacramento, California — **1860**

Southern states secede from the United States; the Civil War breaks out in the U.S (1860-1861) — **1861**

President Lincoln issues the Emancipation Proclamation
The Battle of Gettysburg occurs — **1863**

Civil War ends and slavery is abolished in America; President Lincoln is assassinated
Lewis Carroll publishes *Alice's Adventures in Wonderland* — **1865**

The U.S. buys Alaska for $7.2 million — **1867**

Jules Verne writes *20,000 Leagues Under the Sea*
Campbell Soup company is formed — **1870**

The Statue of Liberty is dedicated in New York Harbor — **1886**

George Eastman invents the Kodak box camera — **1888**

Orville and Wilbur Wright fly the first plane at Kitty Hawk, North Carolina — **1903**

First crossword puzzle appears in the *New York World* newspaper — **1913**

BIBLIOGRAPHY

Bradford, Sarah. **Harriet Tubman: The Moses of Her People.** Carol Publishing Group, New York, 1994.

Douglass, Frederick. **Narrative of the Life of Frederick Douglass, an American Slave, Written by Himself.** Signet, New York, 1968.

McMullan, Kate. **The Story of Harriet Tubman, Conductor of the Underground Railroad.** Bantam, Doubleday, Dell, New York, 1991.

Petry, Ann. **Harriet Tubman: Conductor on the Underground Railroad.** Pocket Books, New York, 1955.